Convert to Rastafari

85 Tips, Principles & Teachings to Convert to Rastafari

By

Empress

Empress

Copyright © 2017 Empress

All rights reserved.

Convert to Rastafari

Rasta Books on Amazon

Empress

Rasta Way of Life

Rastafari Livity Book
Empress Yuajah

Convert to Rastafari

Empress

Convert to Rastafari

Empress

Convert to Rastafari

DEDICATION

For all the Men and Women who aspire to live as Rasta, and embrace the livity to the fullest.
Jah Rastafari.

Table of Contents

What is a Rasta?	14
Beliefs of Rastafari (7)	16
Marcus Garvey: Our Prophet (1)	19
Haile Selassie Teachings (6)	21
#6 Haile Selassie in the Bible	24
Haile Selassie Facts Every Rasta Knows (8)	26
"Rasta to Rasta" code (6)	31
Bob Marley Interview: His Beliefs in Jah Rastafari (1)	40
Bob Marley Interview on Rastafari	41
How to Pray as a Rasta (6)	44
Bible stories about Rastafari (3)	55
Rasta Language: Common words & Phrases (10)	83
Ital Rasta Food Laws (8)	87

Lion of Judah Flag Meaning (5)   91

Meaning of Dreadlocks as Rasta (10)   95

Convert to Rastafari (Vow) (9)   102

How to Choose Your Rasta Name (5)   114

A book titled "Convert to Rastafari?"

Yes, I am aware that one cannot *Convert to Rastafari* as Rastafari is not a Religion. I am Tafari, I am aware. However there are many people today who are becoming aware of "the light of Jah," and seek guidance to live this way of life.

Rastafari is a way of life that acknowledges Jah is some very specific, special and spiritual ways. Why must one go to a bald head for guidance on Rastafari? Why learn the livity from someone who is a student of the livity themselves?

It is my work as Rasta on the Journey, to provide Jah Rastafari guidance to those who seek it. To embrace Rastafari is a blessing. *Convert to Rastafari* is my way of sharing this blessing of my faith, with those who want to embrace it too. The more Rastafari minded individuals we have on the earth, the better the world will be.

Blessed. Love.

Convert to Rastafari

Empress

What is a Rasta?

A Rasta is a person who loves and respects, and is spiritually aware of, the earth, himself, King

Selassie I, Jah, and Jah creations. There are some basic beliefs and principles, that every Rasta lives by, that you

should be aware of, before you convert

to Rastafari.

Empress

Beliefs of Rastafari (7)

#1 Equal Rights and Justice - A Rasta is a person who believes in equal rights and justice for all.

#2 Jah/God - A Rasta is a person who knows Jah is always watching all that we say and do.

#3 Judgement Day - A Rasta is a person who knows each man and woman will be responsible for his and her own judgement by Jah.

#4 To Eat dead flesh is unclean - A Rasta believes the eating of meat/flesh is an unclean act for the body mind and spirit.

#5 Recognize the face of Jah - A Rasta knows, King Selassie I is the face of Jah manifested as man.

#6 The Babylon System - A Rasta is a person who is aware of the Babylon System, (the lies of the Government,) and its effects on humanity.

#7 Respect for nature - A Rasta is a person who has a deep love and respect for all nature, because he knows, Jah is in nature.

Marcus Garvey: Our Prophet (1)

Marcus Garvey, a man of Jamaican Ancestry... a leader, and a speaker, who brought hope & and inspiration to Millions of formerly enslaved Africans, once said "Look to Africa for the crowning of a Black King!"

Marcus Garvey Prophecy comes to pass...

On November 2nd 1930, King Selassie I, was Crowned "King of Ethiopia." From that day forward Marcus Garvey was hailed as a Prophet, to the Rastafari Peoples for his "prophetic words" and the Rastafari "faith" was born.

Convert to Rastafari

Haile Selassie Teachings (6)

You do not have to believe in Haile Selassie to be a Rasta. But, that would be like a Christian who doesn't believe in Christ. King Selassie I has some very important teachings for all humanity. He left them as his legacy here on earth. As Rasta we carry his birth name (RasTafari) and we aim to emulate his beliefs and actions such as unity, spirituality, education and equal rights for all.

Haile Selassie I Quote #1: Sharing with

the poor

"...a way of life in which the blessings and benefits of the modern world can be enjoyed by all."

Haile Selassie I Quote #2: Equality

"..above all, Ethiopia is dedicated to the principle of the equality of all men, irrespective of differences of race, color or creed."

Haile Selassie I Quote #3: Discrimination

"...as we do not practice or permit discrimination within our nation, so we oppose it wherever it is found."

Haile Selassie I Quote #4: Religious Division

"...as we guarantee to each the right to

worship as he chooses, so we denounce the policy which sets man against man on issues of religion."

Haile Selassie I Quote #5 : Racism

"...as we extend the hand of universal brotherhood to all, without regard to race or color, so we condemn any social or political order which distinguishes among God's children on this most specious of ground.

#6 Haile Selassie in the Bible

During the coronation, King Selassie I, was given a new name to represent his new life as King.

he was born RasTafari Makonnen, his coronation name became, *Haile*

Selassie, or might of the Trinity. King Selassie I full crowning title was, "King of Kings, Lord of Lords, Conquering <u>Lion of the Tribe of Judah,</u> elect of God."

King James Bible:

Reference to Haile Selassie

Revelation 5: "Weep not: behold,<u> the Lion of the tribe of Juda,</u> the Root of David, hath prevailed to open the book, and to loose the seven seals thereof."

Convert to Rastafari

Notice how his crowning title matches up to the scripture from revelation 5?

Haile Selassie Facts Every Rasta Knows

(8)

These King Selassie I "facts" are important because again, this is common knowledge amongst Rasta, and often reasoned about in Rastafari circles. Let's get to it.

#1 Haile Selassie Date of Birth: Haile Selassie was born on *July 23rd 1982, his birth name was Tafari Makonnen.*

#2 Haile Selassie Father Name: His father was Ras Makonnen, his mother was Yeshimebet Ali.

#3 Crowned the same time: Both Empress Menen (his wife) and King Selassie I were crowned rulers of Ethiopia, in the same ceremony, at the same time. For this reason, In Rastafari men and women are equal.

Empress

#4 Haile Selassie & Queen Elizabeth: In 1935 Mussolini, Italy invaded Ethiopia. His Majesty Received aid from Queen Elizabeth, of England fight and eventually keep Ethiopia.

#5 King's Faith/Religion: King Selassie

I practiced Ethiopian Coptic Christianity.

#6 His Majesty Donated land to Rasta:

In 1948 King Selassie I donate many hectares of his personal land to Rasta who migrated to Shashemene, Ethiopia. Wikipedia says it was 500 hectares.

Empress

#7 King Selassie I & Time magazine: November 3 1930, The King was on the Front of Time Magazine!

#8 King Selassie I & Dreadlocks: There was a point when King Selassie I was a small child that he had dreadlocks. Rasta love this fact. There are photos of him online with the locks.

#9 Haile Selassie Visit to Jamaica : April 1966 He visited Kingston Jamaica. Rastafari celebrate this day every year and call it "Grounation Day."

#10 Haile Selassie exotic pets: King Selassie I had pet lions in his palace.

"Rasta to Rasta" code (6)

As a natural-born Rasta, and from what I have seen with Rastafari friends, Rasta people are very sensitive. Due to this, we are very considerate regarding how we handle the feelings and thoughts of other people. If you want to become a Rasta, you will have to know how to conduct yourself with other Rasta, as a Rasta.

#1 Rasta as a Rasta code - Love:

Put patience, love, and understanding, at the forefront of your personal dealings and your interactions with other Rasta. Rasta put self-love at the top of our list each day. With this inner love, we can express more outward love. Try to remember the word "love," if and when you ever feel yourself stepping out of line as a Rasta, with another Rasta.

Convert to Rastafari

#2 Rasta as a Rasta code - Unity:

Rasta likes to stand united as one. When in the presence of other Rasta make a special effort to get along. If a Rasta has a different opinion than you, Just let it be. The moment will pass. In Rastafari, it's more important to *stand united as Rasta, than to be right,* and be divided from those of our own faith.

#3 Rasta as a Rasta code - Freedom:

Don't ever tell another Rasta how to be a Rasta. This type of behavior is ridiculous. Only The Most High knows the hearts and minds of people, and only The Most High has the power and the ability to judge. Allow people to embrace Rastafari as they see fit. Some Rasta are at the beginner stages, of the Livity, and will take time to grow into maturity, just as baby grows into adulthood.

#4 Rasta as a Rasta code - Silence:

As a new Rasta you will learn that *silence is Golden.* There are some people who call themself Rasta, who feel it is ok to raise their voice in order to get their opinion heard. If you are in the middle of a disagreement, just keep silent. Change the topic. Rasta does not like noise, and arguments, and negative energy. Also, we know Jah is watching and we do not want to disappoint him, especially in the presence of other

Kings and Queens.

#5 Rasta as a Rasta code - Never put down Jamaica:

I have met 2 "Knowledge Rasta" both born in Jamaica by the way, and both put Jamaica down. Why? I think it's self-hate. Any true Rasta won't talk bad about Jamaica, (or where he/she is from) because we are aware of the special connection between Emperor Haile Selassie and Jamaica. Never put

Jamaica down as Rasta.

#6 Rasta and Rasta code - Greeting and Salutation:

When you meet and greet another Rasta, it is important to show respect, either by saying the word "respect" or, by saying something that refers to Rastafari. Here are examples of words Rasta use to show respect when they meet and greet each other...

- Selassie I

- Bless
- Blessings
- Jah Bless
- Respect
- One Heart
- Love
- One Love
- Rastafari

Love and Respect of the Highest Importance

You will hear Rastafari using these words to greet each other and also to say goodbye to each other. In Rastafari showing love and respect is one of the most important elements of being a "Tafari."

Bob Marley Interview: His Beliefs in Jah Rastafari (1)

Empress

Bob Marley Interview on Rastafari

Bob Marley was a member of <u>Rastafari</u> whose culture was a key element in the development of reggae. Bob Marley became an ardent proponent of Rastafari, taking their music out of the socially deprived areas of Jamaica and onto the international music scene. He once gave the following response, which was typical, to a question put to him during a recorded interview:

Interviewer: "Can you tell the people what it means being a Rastafarian?"

Bob: "*I would say to the people,*

    Be still, and

    know that His Imperial Majesty,

    Emperor Haile Selassie of Ethiopia

    is the Almighty.

    Now, the Bible seh so,

    Babylon newspaper seh so, and

Empress

I and I the children seh so.

Yunno?

So I don't see how much more

reveal our people want..."

Convert to Rastafari

How to Pray as a Rasta (6)

#1 Prayer is not mandatory in Rastafari

I would even go as far as to say, to meditatie is slightly more important, but yet still, not mandatory. Your Actions as a Rasta are much more important, than prayers. Do good deeds...Jah sees and knows all.

#2 Meditation as Prayer

Meditation as Rasta is a form of Prayer Mediation as a Rasta, <u>is mediation and prayer in one as a Rasta.</u> Some Rasta pray/meditate throughout the entire day. Any communication with, or connection to Jah, is like a prayer in Rastafari Livity. If you would like a deeper understanding of meditation as a Rastafari, please read "Rasta meditation handbook." to learn Rasta meditation tips tools and techniques.

Empress

#3 No special prayer pose!

The more deeply you feel the prayer, the more deeply Jah will sense your sincerity. Just remember Jah does not only see you when you pray, he sees you at all times. So, a little prayer won't make much of a difference if the rest of the time, you disrespect his commandments and creations (other people & life forms). Pray to Jah sitting up, pray to Jah lying down on your back,

Empress

pray to Jah on your knees... whatever

works best for you. He is aware of all

things at all times.

#4 Lion of Judah Flag as a Prayer tool

I found I have my best Rasta prayer experiences when I set my Lion of Judah flag out before me. So try setting your flag out somewhere where you can pray with it next to you. Touch it before you begin, and touch it again when you are through giving thanks. Remember the Rasta flag is tribal, and has deep spiritual meaning. *The Red color represents blood shed of the African* people, the green color represents the nature of Africa, and the yellow color represents, the Gold that was stolen out of the land. So it's not a bad idea to lay the flag out when you want to pray to Jah Rastafari.

#5 Rasta morning prayer

Typically a Rasta will say Good Morning to Jah upon waking up, and ask him to bless the day and keep Babylon at bay.

"Good Morning Jah, in the name of His Imperial Majesty, Holy Emmanuel I, King

Selassie I.

I and I give thanks, for the good nights rest and for this blessed morning. May all the land be touched by your presence beauty and power.

Keep I and I protected, give I and I strength to survive another Day. Bless I to maintain a positive loving caring and sharing spirit as I serve you Jah on this day. In the name of King Selassie I, Holy Emmanuel I. Jah Rastafari."

#6 Rasta prayer before eating

As Rasta we always like to thank Jah for providing the food and ask him to bless the food that it may nourish our bodies and provide strength. As Rasta we give thanks in the name of King Selassie I and Empress Menen. or simply say Jah Rastafari.

"Jah, I give thanks for this food. Bless this food Most High, that I and I am about to eat. May it nourish I temple, and give I strength.

In the name of the Most High,

give thanks.

Convert to Rastafari

Jah Rastafari."

Empress

Bible stories about Rastafari (3)

Why is it important to know these bible stories as you Convert to Rastafari? Because all Rasta know these stories and as I have said before you may be approached or invited to reason on these stories. That's how it is in Rastafari.

Any Rasta will tell you...the whole entire King James Version bible is Rastafari. However I could not write this book without including at least *three - five \prominent stories* to show examples of

Rastafari in the King James version bible.

#1"The Birth of Samuel"

A Rastaman from the womb, A Mother's request to Jah (Vow) Fulfilled!

There was a certain man from Ramathaim, a Zuphite[a] from the hill country of Ephraim, whose name was Elkanah son of Jeroham, the son of Elihu, the son of Tohu, the son of Zuph, an Ephraimite. ² He had two wives; one was called Hannah and the other Peninnah. Peninnah had children, but Hannah had none.

Year after year this man went up from his town to worship and sacrifice to the Lord Almighty at Shiloh, where Hophni and Phinehas, the two sons of Eli, were priests of the LORD. ⁴ Whenever the day came for Elkanah to sacrifice, he would give portions of the meat to his wife Peninnah and to all her sons and daughters. ⁵ But to Hannah he gave a double portion because he loved her, and the LORD had closed her womb. ⁶ Because the LORD had closed Hannah's womb, her rival kept provoking her in order to irritate her. ⁷ This went on year after year. Whenever Hannah went up to the house of the Lord, her rival provoked her till she wept and would not eat. ⁸ Her husband Elkanah would say to her, "Hannah, why are you weeping? Why don't you eat? Why are you downhearted? Don't I mean more to you than ten sons?"

Once when they had finished eating and drinking in Shiloh, Hannah stood up. Now Eli the priest was sitting on his chair by the doorpost of the Lord's house.

Convert to Rastafari

In her deep anguish Hannah prayed to the Lord, weeping bitterly. **And she made a vow, saying, "Lord Almighty, if you will only look on your servant's misery and remember me, and not forget your servant but give her a son, then I will give him to the Lord for all the days of his life, and no razor will ever be used on his head."**

As she kept on praying to the Lord, Eli observed her mouth. [13] Hannah was praying in her heart, and her lips were moving but her voice was not heard. Eli thought she was drunk [14] and said to her, "How long are you going to stay drunk? Put away your wine."

"Not so, my lord," Hannah replied, "I am a woman who is deeply troubled. I have not been drinking wine or beer; I was pouring out my soul to the L<small>ORD</small>. [16] Do not take your servant for a wicked woman; I have been praying here out of my great anguish and grief."

Eli answered, "Go in peace, and may the God of Israel grant you what you have asked of him."

She said, "May your servant find favor in your eyes." Then she went her way and ate something, and her face was no longer downcast.

Early the next morning they arose and worshiped before the Lord and then went back to their home at Ramah. Elkanah made love to his wife Hannah, and the Lord remembered her. **So in the course of time Hannah became pregnant and gave birth to a son. She named him Samuel,[b] saying, "Because I asked the Lord for him."**

#2 the story of Samson and Delilah

This is the story of a Rastaman, faithful to Jah, and full of strength. One day he breaks Jah commandments by sleeping with a prostitute, and falling in love with a from out of town woman and he loses all.

One day Samson went to Gaza, where he saw a prostitute. He went in to spend the night with her. The people of Gaza were told, "Samson is here!" So they surrounded the place and lay in wait for him all night at the city gate. They made no move during the night, saying, "At dawn we'll kill him."

But Samson lay there only until the middle of the night. Then he got up and took hold of the doors of the city gate, together with the two posts, and tore them loose, bar and all. He lifted them to his shoulders and carried them to the top of the hill that faces Hebron.

Sometime later, he fell in love with a woman in the Valley of Sorek whose name was Delilah. **5** The rulers of the Philistines went to her and said, "See if you can lure him into showing you the secret of his great strength and how we can overpower him so we may tie him up and subdue him. Each one of us will give you eleven hundred shekels[a] of silver."

So Delilah said to Samson, "Tell me the secret of your great strength and how you can be tied up and subdued."

Samson answered her, "If anyone ties me with seven fresh bowstrings that have not been dried, I'll become as weak as any other man."

Then the rulers of the Philistines brought her seven fresh bowstrings that had not been dried, and she tied him with them. **9** With men hidden in the room, she called to him, "Samson, the Philistines are upon you!" But he snapped the bowstrings as easily as a piece of string snaps when it comes close to a flame. So the secret of his strength was not discovered.

Then Delilah said to Samson, "You have made a fool of me; you lied to me. Come now, tell me how you can be tied."

He said, "If anyone ties me securely with new ropes that have never been used, I'll become as weak as any other man."

So Delilah took new ropes and tied him with them. Then, with men hidden in the room, she called to him, "Samson, the Philistines are upon you!" But he snapped the ropes off his arms as if they were threads.

Delilah then said to Samson, "All this time you have been making a fool of me and lying to me. Tell me how you can be tied."

He replied, "If you weave the seven braids of my head into the fabric on the loom and tighten it with the pin, I'll become as weak as any other man." So while he was sleeping, Delilah took the seven braids of his head, wove them into the fabric and tightened it with the pin.

Again she called to him, "Samson, the Philistines are upon you!" He awoke from his sleep and pulled up the pin and the loom, with the fabric.

Then she said to him, "How can you say, 'I love you,' when you won't confide in me? This is the third time you have made a fool of me and haven't told me the secret of your great strength." With such nagging she prodded him day after day until he was sick to death of it.

So he told her everything. "No razor has ever been used on my head," he said, "because I have been a Nazirite dedicated to God from my mother's womb. If my head were shaved, my strength would leave me, and I would become as weak as any other man."

When Delilah saw that he had told her everything, she sent word to the rulers of the Philistines, "Come back once more; he has told me everything." So the rulers of the Philistines returned with the silver in their hands. After putting him to sleep on her lap, she called for someone to shave off the seven locks of his hair, and so began to subdue him. And his strength left him.

Then she called, "Samson, the Philistines are upon you!"

He awoke from his sleep and thought, "I'll go out as before and shake myself free." But he did not know that the LORD had left him.

Then the Philistines seized him, gouged out his eyes and took him down to Gaza. Binding him with bronze shackles, they set him to grinding grain in the prison. But the hair on his head began to grow again after it had been shaved.

The Death of Samson

Now the rulers of the Philistines assembled to offer a great sacrifice to

Dagon their god and to celebrate,

saying, "Our god has delivered Samson,

our enemy, into our hands."

When the people saw him, they praised

their god, saying,

"Our god has delivered our enemy

  into our hands,

the one who laid waste our land

  and multiplied our slain."

While they were in high spirits, they

shouted, "Bring out Samson to entertain

us." So they called Samson out of the prison, and he performed for them.

When they stood him among the pillars, Samson said to the servant who held his hand, "Put me where I can feel the pillars that support the temple, so that I may lean against them." Now the temple was crowded with men and women; all the rulers of the Philistines were there, and on the roof were about three thousand men and women watching Samson perform. Then Samson prayed to the Lord, "Sovereign Lord, remember me. Please, God, strengthen me just once more, and let me with one blow get revenge on the Philistines for my two eyes." Then Samson reached toward the two central pillars on which the temple stood. Bracing himself against them, his right hand on the one and his left hand on the other, Samson said, "Let me die with the Philistines!" Then he pushed with all his might, and down came the temple on the rulers and all the people in it. Thus he killed many more when he died than while he lived.

Then his brothers and his father's whole family went down to get him. They brought him back and buried him between Zorah and Eshtaol in the tomb of Manoah his father. He had led Israel twenty years.

"Despite his having the Spirit of the Lord upon him, his sexual yearnings of

the flesh controlled his life (<u>1 John 2:16</u>)."

#3 King Solomon (Son of King David)

Rasta man turns away from Jah, through females who are not of the same faith

But King Solomon loved many foreign women, as well as the daughter of Pharaoh: women of the Moabites, Ammonites, Edomites, Sidonians, and Hittites— ² from the nations of whom the Lord had said to the children of Israel, **"You shall not intermarry with them, nor they with you. Surely they will turn away your hearts after their gods."** Solomon clung to these in love. ³ **And he had seven hundred wives, princesses, and three**

hundred concubines; and his wives turned away his heart. ⁴ **For it was so, when Solomon was old, that his wives turned his heart after other gods;** and his heart was not loyal to the LORD his God, as was the heart of his father David. ⁵ For Solomon went after Ashtoreth the goddess of the Sidonians, and after Milcom the abomination of the Ammonites. ⁶ Solomon did evil in the sight of the LORD, and did not fully follow the

Lord, as did his father David. ⁷ Then Solomon built a high place for Chemosh the abomination of Moab, on the hill that is east of Jerusalem, and for Molech the abomination of the people of Ammon. ⁸ And he did likewise for all his foreign wives, who burned incense and sacrificed to their gods.

⁹ So the Lord became angry with Solomon, because his heart had turned from the Lord God of

Israel, who had appeared to him twice, ¹⁰ and had commanded him concerning this thing, that he should not go after other gods; but he did not keep what the LORD had commanded. ¹¹ Therefore the LORD said to Solomon, "Because you have done this, and have not kept My covenant and My statutes, which I have commanded you, I will surely tear the kingdom away from you and give it to your servant. [12] Nevertheless I will not do it in your days, for the sake of your father David; I will tear it out of the hand of your son. [13] However I will not tear away the whole kingdom; I will give one tribe to your son for the sake of My servant David, and for the sake of Jerusalem which I have chosen."

Rasta Language: Common words & Phrases (10)

Learning the words of Rasta is easy,

what makes it a little tricky to learn, is hearing these words in an accent we are not used to, such as English, Virgin Islands, American etc.. Enjoy.

Rasta Language is spiritual

Rasta have our own way of speaking because we have our own way of thinking and looking at things. So, The word *Zion* is a Rasta word, but it's not Jamaican Patois. The words *Likkle* more, is Jamaican but it's not Rastafari. Rastafari words and language typically have a spiritual purpose of *blessing*, *condemnation, or identification,* as holy or unholy.

#1 - "Ital" – Clean and Natural as in "Ital food"

#2 -"Blessed Love" – Have a pleasant day.

#3 -"Zion" = Heaven/Ethiopia

#4 -"Jah" = God, The Most High

#5 -"Bless Up" – "Think Positive!" or "Whats up?"

#6 -"Up Up" – A spiritual blessing of positive energy, a Rasta way of greeting another.

#7 -"Fyah Bun" – "Get rid of that, it is of Babylon." or " Get rid of that, it is of

Satan!" (denouncement)

#8 -"Judgement" – God's' wrath upon a group of people or person.

#9 -"Youths" – "Children" or "youth"

#10 -"King" – "Rastaman" or "King Selassie I." "A man with great spiritual wisdom."

#11 -"Queen"/"Empress" – "A Rasta woman," or "a woman of great spiritual wisdom."

#12 -"I and I" – "Me in the Physical... and Me in the spiritual..." (people are very mislead about this Rasta phrase)

#13 -"Jah Rastafari" – "God" & "King Selassie I." Rastafari as the spirituality or Jah in spirit.

#14 -"HIM" – "His Imperial Majesty, Haile Selassie I"

#15 -"Give thanks" – "Give thanks to the creator for he is good." or "Thank you."

#16 -"Babylon" – "Hell/This World/An Authority figure of Babylon."

#17 -"Yes I" - How a Rasta acknowledges another Rasta. A show of spiritual Respect.

Ital Rasta Food Laws (8)

Rasta have laws concerning everything,

but the one that most people seem to be most curious about is how we eat. Here are 10 Ital food laws for you to get familiar with as a new Rasta.

#1 - organic food - Rasta like to eat, food that grows naturally. On a tree, out of the ground, without, pesticides etc. In other words, not created by synthetic seeds etc. or forced to grow.

#2 - No meat! - Rasta do not eat meat, this includes, beef, goat, pork, Chicken,....No shellfish because they clean the bottom of the sea, therefor, shellfish are unclean for Rasta to eat. For modern day Rasta, not eating meat, means not eating anything that was alive and is now dead.

#3 - No preservatives - Preservatives cause Cancer in the human body. Google it!

#4 - Only natural sugars - Rasta love

to enjoy natural sweeteners, such as honey, molasses or cane sugar.

#5 - No salt - Rasta prefer to cook without salt. If we must use salt we use sea salt. Himalayan salt is even better, it is packed with minerals the body needs.

#6 - No Fish - Most Rastas have stopped eating fish nowadays, simply because of how fish are raised/farmed.

#7 - No Eggs - This depends on the individual Rasta. Some Rasta still eat eggs. I eat eggs about once a month for the nutritional value, because of my already vegan Ital Diet, and the fact that I am a woman of menstruation age.

#8 - No alcohol - No beer, no wine, no liquor. Rasta do not make his holy temple drunk or Jah will not come inside.

#9 - No White food - Rasta eat white food in moderation. (white bread, white pasta, white pastries, white rice, white potatoes etc.) These foods fill you up, but lack nutritional value for the body.

Rasta Conscious food Choices

The Ital food laws are mostly for you to keep in mind as you pick and choose your food at the grocery store, as a new Rasta. As time goes by you will automatically know which foods to stay away from, and which foods you can eat in moderation. That is really how we Rasta eat...with awareness, and with consciousness.

Lion of Judah Flag Meaning (5)

Lion of Judah Flag Keywords

Here is a list of keywords associated spiritually, with the Lion of Judah Flag.

- Victory

- Love
- Unity
- Jah (God)
- Strength
- Royalty
- King Selassie I

Test Questions: Lion of Judah Flag

Common knowledge among Rasta concerning the Lion of Judah Flag. To Convert to Rastafari you will need to know this at all times.

1. **What are the Colors of the Rastafari Flag?** - Red Yellow and green (and Gold).

2. **What is the name of the lion on the front of the flag?** - The lion of The Tribe of Judah.

3. **List 3 word associations of the Rastafari Flag?** - Love, unity, strength,

4. **What country in Africa does the Rastafari Flag Represent?** - Ethiopia.

5. **Who does the Lion on the Flag Represent?** - Haile Selassie of Ethiopia.

Convert to Rastafari

Meaning of Dreadlocks as Rasta (10)

Like a practicing Sikh who wears his silver bracelet on his wrist, or a Christian who wears a cross pendent from his necklace. Rasta wear Dreadlocks as a symbol of his faith and commitment to jah Rastafari.

Convert to Rastafari

Dreadlocks have 3 Basic Meanings

1. *Commitment* to Jah Rastafari as a physical representation of a vow.

2. *Love and Unity* with Mother Earth and Jah creations.

3. *Spiritual awareness* of life, and natural living.

How to Wash Rasta Dreadlocks

Dreadlocks may be washed any way the Rasta desires. But if you choose to go natural, which as a Rasta we embrace, you want to buy a 100% natural shampoo. Some Rasta like to wash their hair strictly with Salt water as they do in the Caribbean, the salt water helps the hair to lock too. Personally I use shampoo.

You might want to check out....

- Dr. Bronner's pure castile soap (peppermint)

- Dreadlocks Naturally on etsy. I have heard good things about it.

The type of Shampoo you need right now, will depend on which stage you are at in the locking process.

How to make Dreadlocks lock faster!

You may also opt to create a mixture of aloe and lime juice, which will help the locks to lock up. This works well for people will straight or loose curl types.

Or this mixture may also be used for African tightly coiled hair/beginner locks. This mixture will lock up locks fast and neat. Blocking any possibility of loose stray hairs. Use it after you finish washing your locks, while hair is still damp.

Convert to Rastafari (Vow) (9)

Many people wonder how and why a Rastafari behaves different from others. Why there are things he just won't do.....here is an idea of the promises a Rastaman or woman has on his/her heart. As you speak your vow, you will too. You may read this vow. Once a week to remind yourself why you became a Rastafari.

#1 ...not to be defined by society or any one individual

Rastafari is a way of living that embraces individuality. We know Babylon tries to make us all think act and dress the same way. But, we as Rasta know better. Jah made every individual unique. We define ourselves and do not allow ourselves to be defined by Babylon or any particular individual.

#2 ...to be a creative free thinking human being

As Rastafarians we embrace creative free thinking. It is through creative free thinking that Jah (The Most High) can communicate with us. In Rastafari we believe each man should live his life as he chooses doing the things he enjoys doing, and that each individual has a unique contribution to make to society. We know we are not clones or zombies, for Babylon.

#3 ...to have spiritual awareness...

Convert to Rastafari

It is important to live life as a spiritual being. Spiritual awareness allows a person to feel whole, and complete in this ever-changing, ever shifting, ever bustling society. One needs time to "still the mind" and just allow the body to be.

Through spirituality (prayer meditation and fasting) Rastafarians receive inner strength to deflect the corruption and pressures of today's society

#4 ...to approach all disagreements and misunderstanding with love...
To be a Rasta means, that in any disagreement, and or misunderstanding we want to try to view the situation from a loving and understanding point of view once we get some time alone.

With this in mind we try to be the first one to give in or to apologize. We know Jah is watching and we must be on our best behaviour to enter Zion

#5 ...to have a spiritual rebirth in the truth

Rastafarians follow the way of life of spiritual truth. I can assure you this way of life is positive and good for everyone because Rasta are born with this awareness and knowledge that Rastafari is the rightful way. Now I walk in

spiritual truth

**#6 ...not seek to define
/dislike/discriminate against
others....**

Rasta knows Babylon is full of many

judgements. Rasta knows all people are

equal in the eyes of Jah. For this reason

it is ungodly behaviour to define

another person based on their birth

country, class, ethnic background or

skin color. We think in terms of love, not the terms that Babylon has used to divide people today. Rasta take the high road, we choose not to participate in thoughtless, competitive, unloving behaviour.

#7 ...to unite in love and harmony with others whose mission is peace and love...

Empress

It is of the utmost importance that Rasta interacts with one another in a loving positive way. Other Rasta's become like your brothers and sisters once you begin to follow this way of life. We are a very close-knit loving community. This means...

Sharing freely from the heart and expecting nothing in return

Having a mentality of equality not competition among other Rasta

Quietly being able to agree to disagree without acknowledgement from the other person.

Staying away from negative comments or discussions that cause confusion and or division among Rasta

#8 ...life is determined by the daily choices that I make...

Rastafari man and Rastafari Women enjoy freedom and to own our own lives. We take responsibility for our own happiness by the choices that we make daily. Rasta knows that Jah gave us "free will", so now it is our job to wake up every day with our chosen purpose in mind.

#9 ...to be open to Jah Guidance and love

Rasta men and women allow The Most High to communicate with them and guide them towards endeavours that are productive and loving. Let Jah be your guide, just open your heart.

Empress

How to Choose Your Rasta Name (5)

To convert to Rastafari you will need a new name. It represents a new spiritual beginning, with Jah Rastafari as your mentor.

5 Tips to create Your Rasta Name

1. Choose your Rasta name straight from the Bible

2. Make up a Rasta name by using some Jamaican Patois words

3. Put the word "Ras" in front of your birth name if you are a male, put the Word "Empress" or "Queen" in front of your birth name if you are

a female.

4. Use a word that is part of Rastafari Culture (Jah, Trinity, Haile, Lion, etc)

5. Mix up these options

To learn more about the [Rasta Way of Life](), read the Ebook on amazon.com

Zion	Highly/Heights
Royal	Roots
Kingly	Mystic/Mystical
Tafari	Natty
Menen	Unity
David	Lion
Prophet	Truth
Trinity	Jah

The word "Empress" for Rasta Woman....

I put the word "Empress" in front of my Rasta name to Emulate the name of Empress Menen. In Rastafari Culture most Rasta women like to put the word

"Queen" in front of their Rasta name. I like Empress because it sounds more Icient to me.

Rasta men are named "Kings...."

Rasta men are naturally called "King." Some prefer the word "Ras" in front of their Rasta name, meaning "Prince" or "head." Again it is a personal Choice.

Blessed Love.

The word "Empress" for Rasta Woman....
I put the word "Empress" in front of my Rasta name to Emulate the name of Empress Menen. In Rastafari Culture most Rasta women like to put the word "Queen" in front of their Rasta name. I like Empress because it sounds more Icient to me.
Rasta men are named "Kings...."

Rasta men are naturally called "King." Some prefer the word "Ras" in front of their Rasta name, meaning "Prince" or "head." Again it is a personal Choice. Blessed Love.

ABOUT THE AUTHOR

Empress has been a Rastafari since birth. She lives with her Rastafari Family and enjoys writing music, and Rastafari Books.
www.jamaicanrastafarianlove.com

Rasta Livity Books on Amazon.com

Jah Rastafari Prayers

Convert to Rastafari

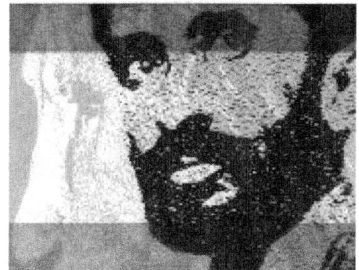

Rasta Way of Life

Life as a Rasta Woman

Convert to Rastafari

Rasta Rules
144 Rastafarian Rules, Laws and Regulations

Empress

Empress Rasta Principles: for Wife & Mother

Blessed Love.

Printed in Great Britain
by Amazon